ACKNOWLEDGEMENTS

Pattern Editor and Production ....
Text Editor...
Art Assistant .... Robert Huffman
Typesetting and Layout .... Steve Campbell, Janet Moore
County Magazine Printshop Ltd.
Colour Photography .... Randy and Judy Wardell

We have dedicated this book to the memory of Frank DeSouza, a good friend and inspiration.

PREFACE

To protect ourselves against "Mother Nature's" sometimes hostile environment, it is often necessary to enclose our living and working areas with walls.

The earliest cave dwellers recognized the necessity for wall decorations by painting art directly on their walls.

The goal of this book is to explore the subject of stained glass clocks, mirrors and picture frames as functional, decorative art for the office or our living spaces.

Included in this collection of patterns are some traditional and simple patterns within the skill level of a beginning craftsperson as well as some intricate and challenging constructions for a more skilled crafter. Many of the projects can be adapted for use as either a clock, mirror or picture frame with only minor alterations to the pattern.

A photographic special instruction guide has been included to assist you in coping with possible problem areas. A step by step outline offers a general guide for construction.

We hope that you will find many hours of enjoyment while constructing these projects and trust that the wide range of subjects fulfill the requests and needs of your friends and family.

Judy & Randy Wardell

Canadian Cataloguing in Publication Data
Wardell, Judy, 1956-
    Stained glass wall decorations
ISBN 0-919985-03-3.
1. Glass painting and staining. 2. Glass craft - Patterns.
I. Wardell, Randy A. (Randy Allan), 1954- . II. Title.
TT298.W375 1985   748.8   C85-098070-4

Printed in Canada

CONTENTS

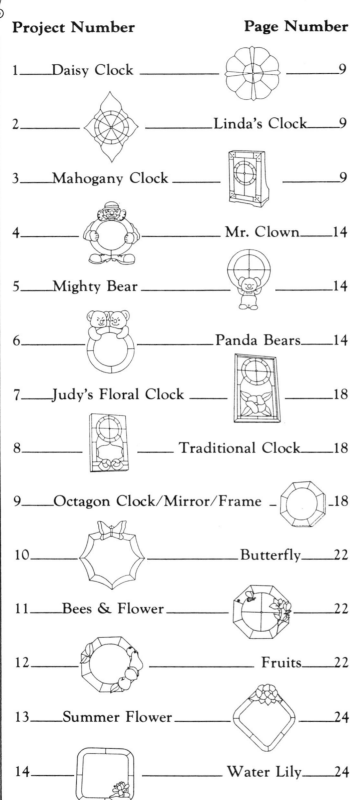
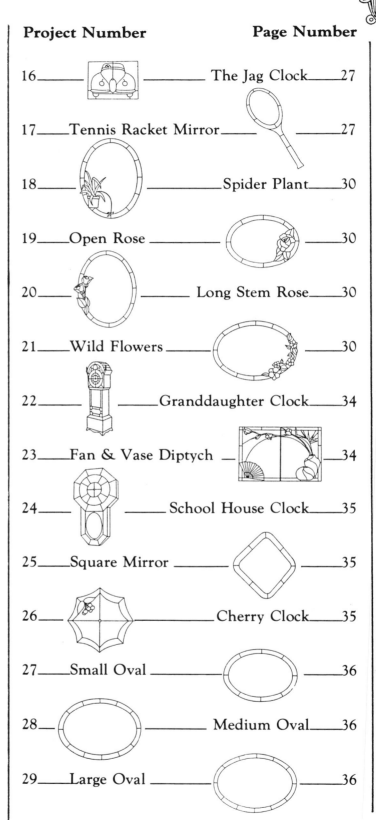
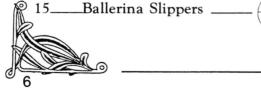

GENERAL INSTRUCTION

This set of instructions is complete, yet abbreviated due to lack of space. For more complete information on foil assembly techniques, refer to other Wardell Publication books.

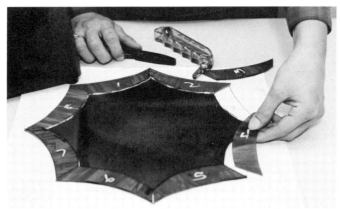

1. Trace patterns making two copies: one will be cut up for your pattern pieces, the other will be your assembly guide. Carefully cut out your glass pieces and place them on your guide as you go. You must be sure your glass pieces fit together properly. This may require some grinding.

2. When the fit accurately matches the assembly guide, carefully wrap them with copper foil. Be sure to press the foil to the glass using a wood lathkin. Secure the glass pieces with horseshoe nails around the outside edge. Solder the panel on front and back side.

3. It is important when assembling a project that has edge sides to join the corners correctly. The patterns are designed so the corners meet as shown in the photo rather than a butt end style.

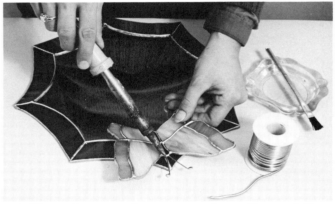

4. To apply an overlay you must have all parts fully soldered and cleaned. Position the overlays as shown in the project illustration. Carefully apply a SMALL amount of flux to each joint and solder securely in place.

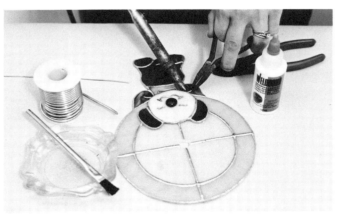

5. Many of the projects require solder or wire detail. Refer to your full size pattern, cut and shape the wires as required. If it cannot be soldered, glue in place with white glue.

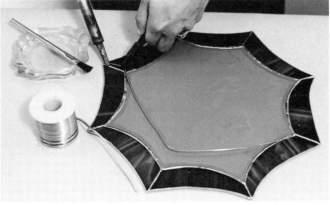

6. You must securely attach a hanging wire to the back of your project by soldering it along a seam. First determine where the balance point is, cut the wire to proper length and solder as shown.

SPECIAL INSTRUCTION
CLOCKS

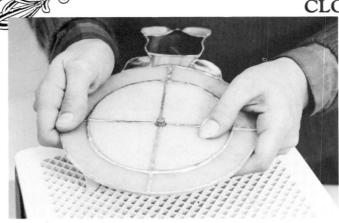 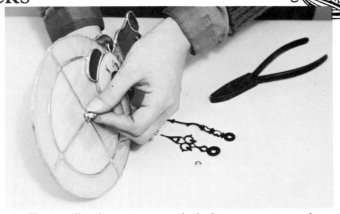

1. If you have access to a grinder with a ¼" bit, the most accurate way to fit the clock movement shaft is to use it to increase the hole size for a proper fit. If a grinder is not available, be sure the hole is large enough before soldering clock face together.

2. To install a battery operated clock movement, simply insert shaft from the back, place on metal washer then secure in place with locknut provided. Next, place on clock hands in the proper order, starting with hour hand then the minute hand and finally the locknut.

MIRRORS

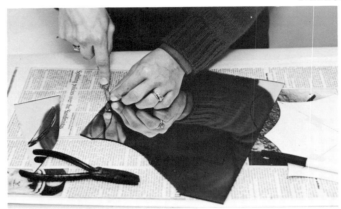 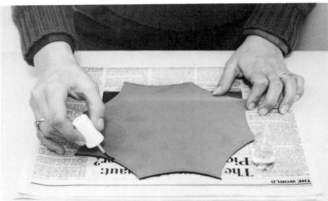

1. To protect the mirror back from scratches while cutting, always place your mirror on a clean work surface. (We use several thicknesses of newspaper.) Mirror silvering will chip easily when breaking out a score so use pliers with caution. Try to avoid grinding the edge, however, if you must, always grind with the back facing you and never lay the piece directly on grinder table surface.

2. To help in preventing the *"Cursed Black Edge"* caused when the exposed edge comes into contact with corrosive agents, protect the edge before foiling by applying clear nail polish (or varnish) to all edges. Carefully apply the flux to avoid getting it on any exposed mirror back surface.

PICTURE FRAMES

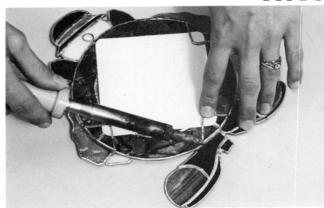 

1. To allow for easy placement and removal of your picture in your frame, solder glass triangles in each corner on the back. You must place a cardboard spacer between the triangle clip and the frame surface. Mount your picture to a piece of bristol board and place into frame.

2. For a permanent installation of your picture into the frame, cut two pieces of clear glass (single strength) and sandwich your picture inside. Foil these pieces together as if they were one piece, then solder into frame.

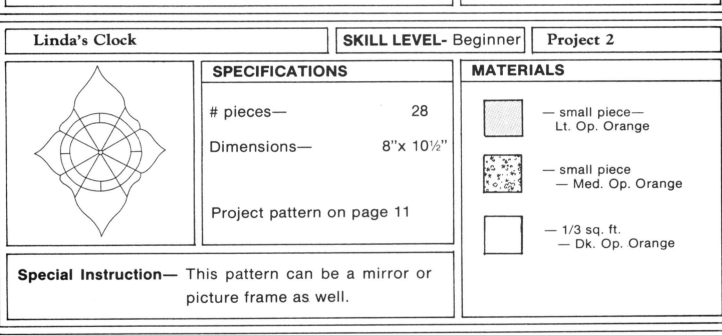

Daisy Clock

SKILL LEVEL- Beginner | **Project 1**

SPECIFICATIONS

# pieces—	20
Dimensions—	11"x 11"

Project pattern on page 10

MATERIALS

— 1-1/3 sq. ft.
— Lt. Purple Opal

— ¼ sq. ft.
— Dk. Purple Opal

Special Instruction— The outside petals on this project slant back slightly.

Linda's Clock

SKILL LEVEL- Beginner | **Project 2**

SPECIFICATIONS

# pieces—	28
Dimensions—	8"x 10½"

Project pattern on page 11

MATERIALS

— small piece—
Lt. Op. Orange

— small piece
— Med. Op. Orange

— 1/3 sq. ft.
— Dk. Op. Orange

Special Instruction— This pattern can be a mirror or picture frame as well.

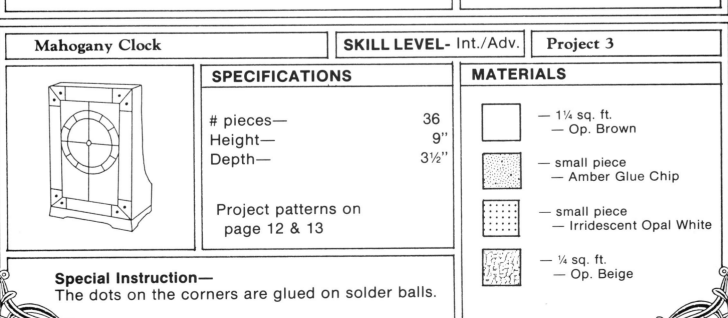

Mahogany Clock

SKILL LEVEL- Int./Adv. | **Project 3**

SPECIFICATIONS

# pieces—	36
Height—	9"
Depth—	3½"

Project patterns on
page 12 & 13

MATERIALS

— 1¼ sq. ft.
— Op. Brown

— small piece
— Amber Glue Chip

— small piece
— Irridescent Opal White

— ¼ sq. ft.
— Op. Beige

Special Instruction—
The dots on the corners are glued on solder balls.

Project 1

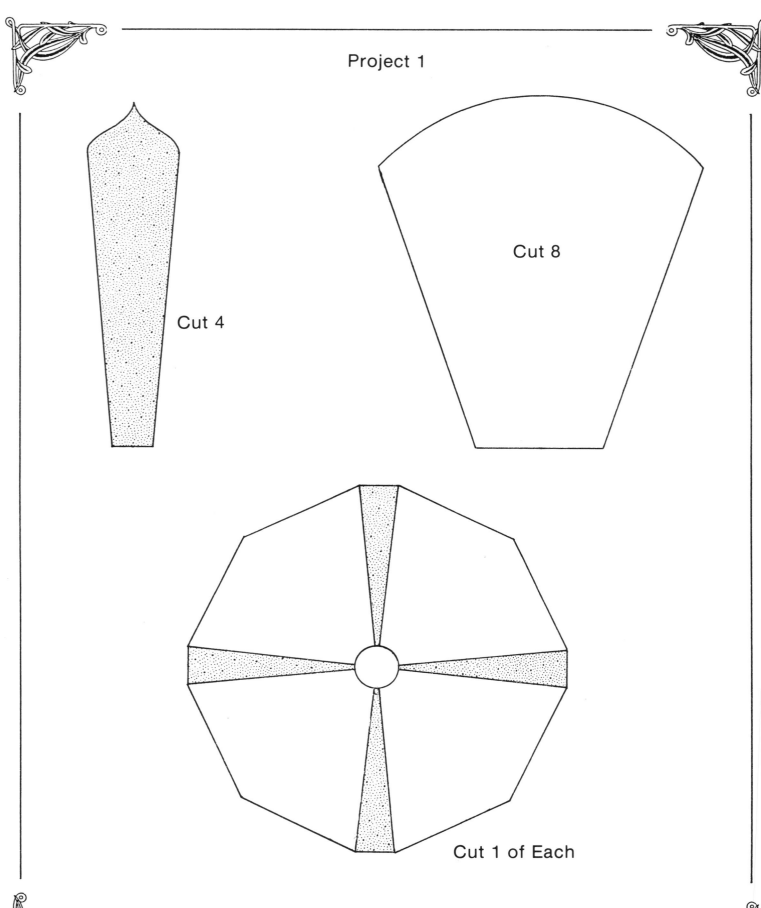

Cut 4

Cut 8

Cut 1 of Each

Project 2

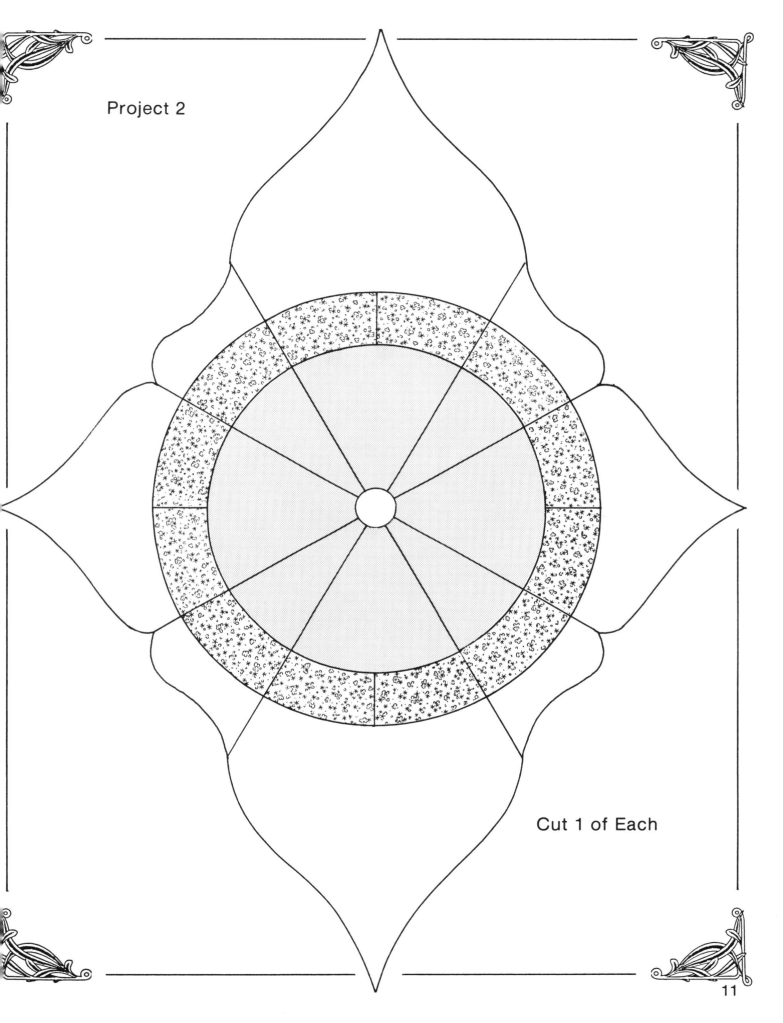

Cut 1 of Each

11

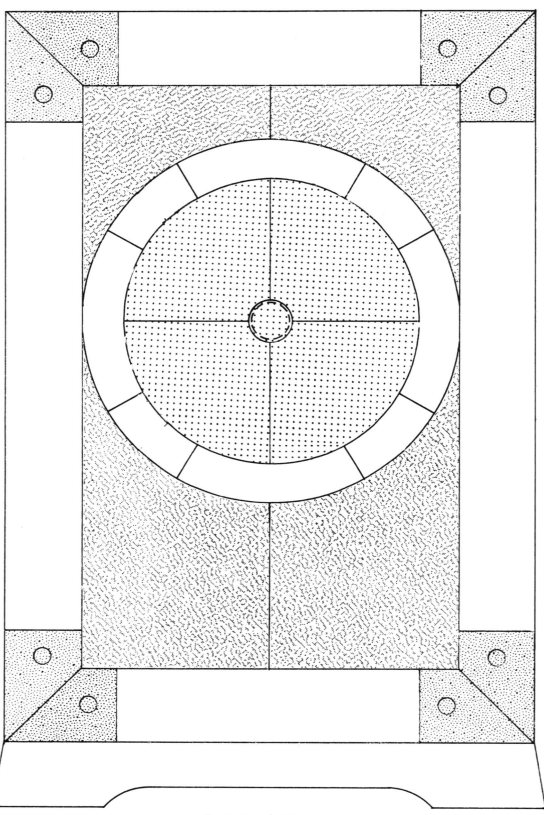

Cut 1 of Each

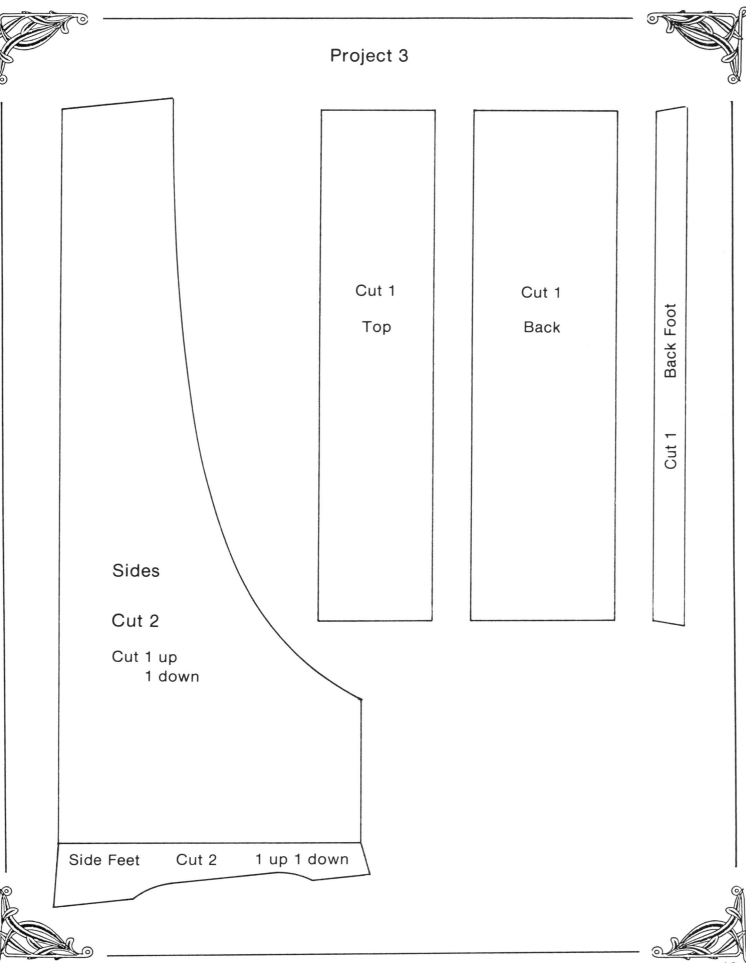

Cut 1

Top

Cut 1

Back

Back Foot

Cut 1

Sides

Cut 2

Cut 1 up
1 down

Side Feet   Cut 2   1 up 1 down

Mr. Clown

SPECIFICATIONS

# pieces—	26
Dimensions—	7½"x 9"

Project pattern on page 15

MATERIALS

- — small piece— Op. Yellow
- — small piece— Op. Orange
- — small piece— Op. White
- — small piece— Black
- — small piece— Dk. Op. Orange
- — ¼ sq. ft.— Yellow/Orange Confetti
- — small piece— Op. Red
- — small piece— Op. Green

½"— Red Faceted Jewel

Special Instruction—
This project can also be a clock or mirror. Refer to colour picture for glass and wire overlay positioning.

Mighty Bear

SPECIFICATIONS

# pieces—	17
Dimensions—	6½"x 9"

Project pattern on page 16

MATERIALS

- — ½ sq. ft.— Op. Yellow

Clock Center— 5½"x 5½"— Lt. Op. Yellow

- — small piece— Beige
- — small piece— Lt. Opal Blue
- — small piece— Dk. Opal Blue
- — small piece— Op. Brown

Globs— 1 small— Black

Special Instruction—
This project can also be a mirror or picture frame. For an additional project, solder Panda Bears to top of this project.

Panda Bears

SPECIFICATIONS

# Pieces—	14
Dimensions—	7"x 9½"

Project pattern on page 17

MATERIALS

 — ½ sq. ft.— Strky Red Opal

5½ x 5½" — Mirror

 — sm. piece — Black

 — sm. piece — White

Globs — 2 small — Black

Special Instruction—
This project can also be a clock or picture frame
— Lines on face, ears, paws are wire overlays
— Eyes are glued on solder beads

Cut 1 of Each

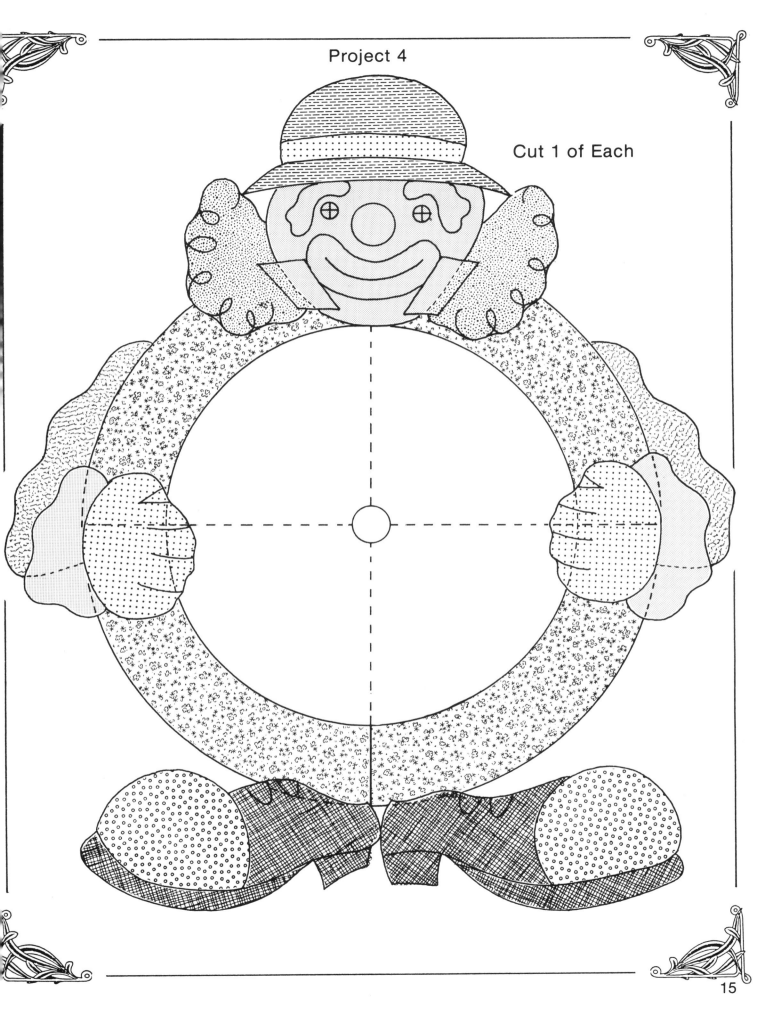

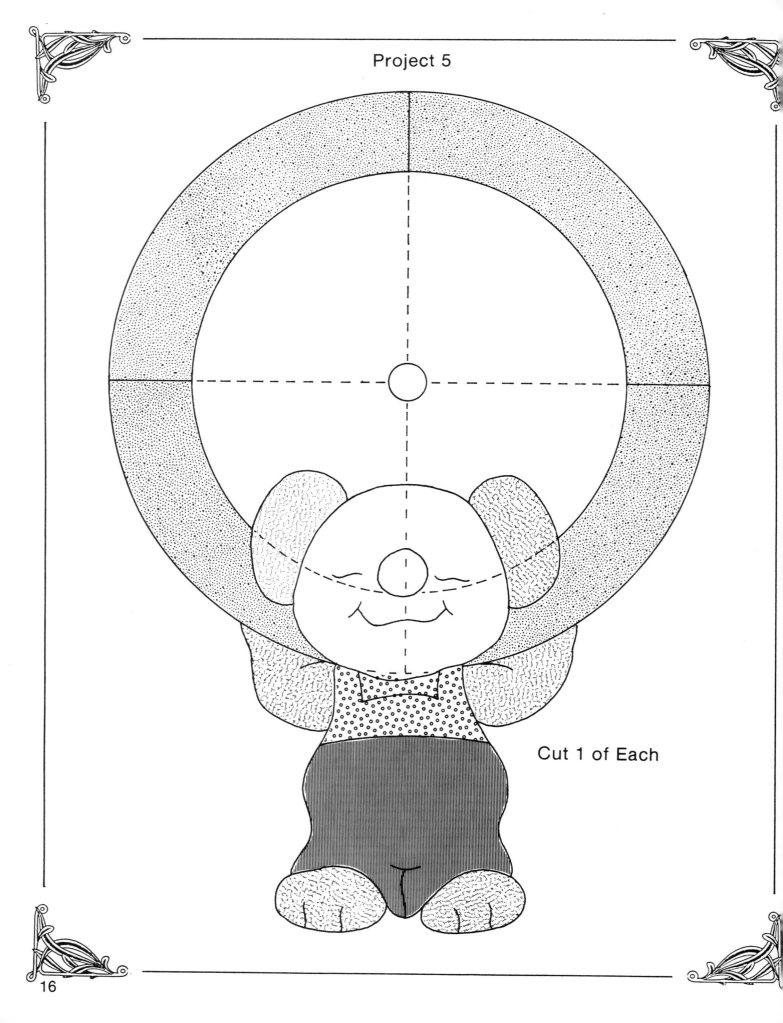

Project 5

Cut 1 of Each

16

Project 6

Cut 1
of Each

Judy's Floral Clock	SKILL LEVEL- Int./Adv.	Project 7

SPECIFICATIONS

Pieces— 43

Dimensions— 9½"x 15"

Project patterns on pages 19 & 20

MATERIALS

- — 1 sq. ft.— Op. Beige
- — ¼ sq. ft.— Opal Red
- — ¼ sq. ft.— Strky Op. Red
- — ¾ sq. ft.— Op. Strky Brown
- — ¼ sq. ft.— Op. Green
- — small piece— Op. Yellow

Special Instruction— This project is best supported by a wood frame or if desired construct a 1½" glass border around all sides (see below).

Traditional Clock	SKILL LEVEL- Int./Adv.	Project 8

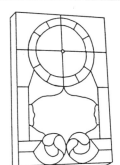

SPECIFICATIONS

Pieces— 43

Dimensions— 9½"x 15"

Clock movement requires pendulum

Project patterns on pages 19 & 21

MATERIALS

- — 1 sq. ft.— Dk. Op. Green
- — 1 sq. ft.— Op. White
- — small piece — Op. Yellow
- — ¼ sq. ft.— Cath. Green
- — 6 x 7½" — Antique Clear

Special Instruction— This project is best supported by a wood frame or if desired construct a 1½" glass border around all sides (see diagram).

Octagon Clock/Mirror/Frame	SKILL LEVEL- Beginner	Project 9

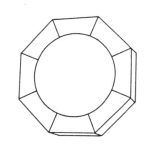

SPECIFICATIONS

Pieces— clock— 12
mirror— 9

Dimensions— 10¼"x 10¼"

NOTE: Project pattern is on insert page. Use top section of school house clock.

MATERIALS

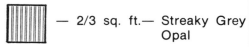 — 2/3 sq. ft.— Streaky Grey Opal

(Border)

— 9"x 9" — White opal or mirror or clear

Special Instruction— To make the pattern for the clock/mirror/picture frame, trace only top section of School house clock on insert sheet.

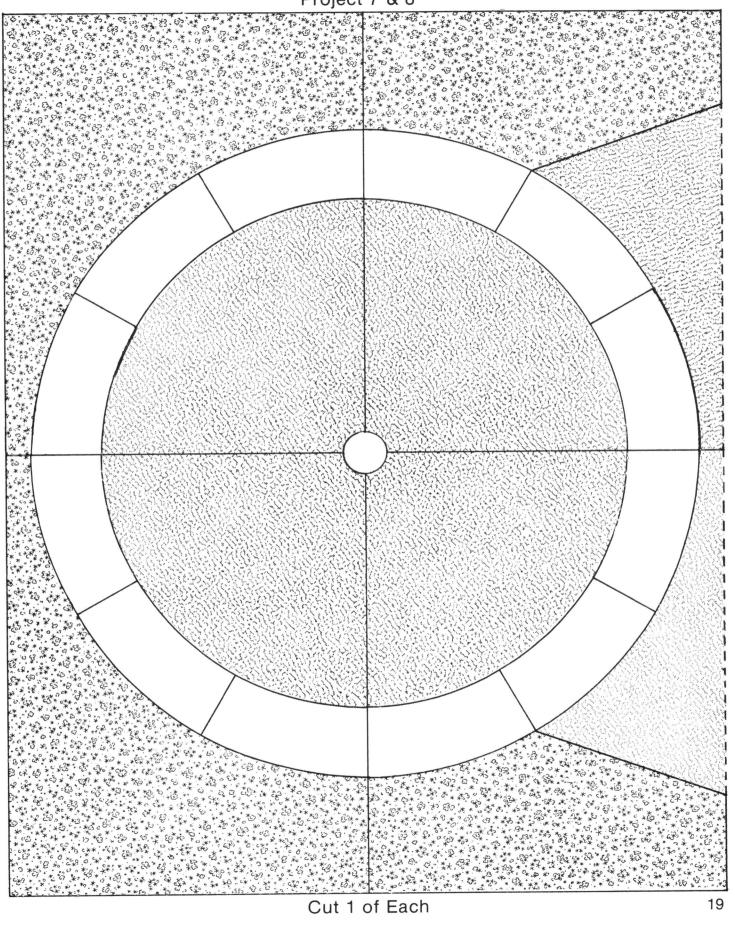

Cut 1 of Each

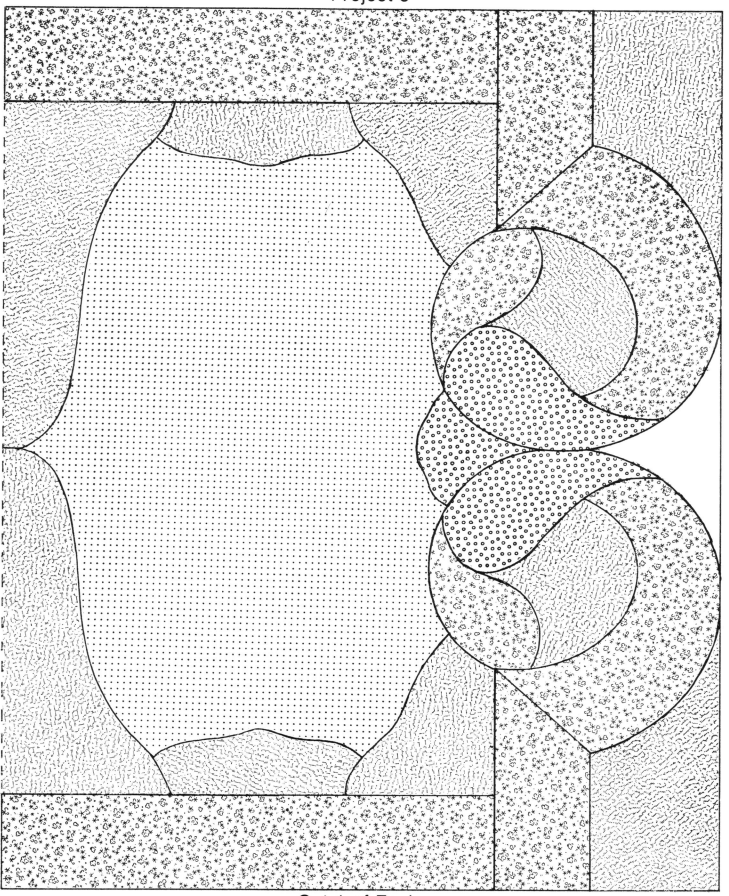

Cut 1 of Each

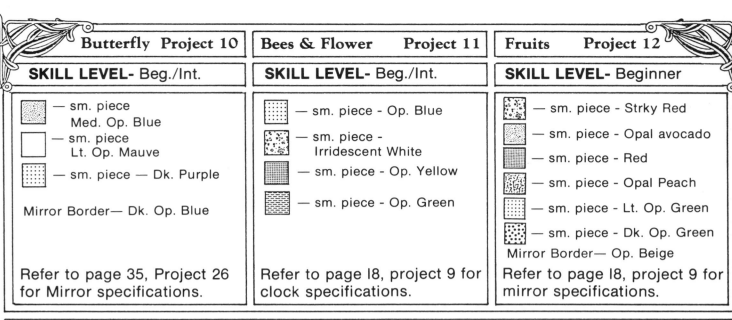

SKILL LEVEL- Beg./Int. | **SKILL LEVEL-** Beg./Int. | **SKILL LEVEL-** Beginner

— sm. piece Med. Op. Blue
— sm. piece Lt. Op. Mauve
— sm. piece — Dk. Purple

Mirror Border— Dk. Op. Blue

Refer to page 35, Project 26 for Mirror specifications.

— sm. piece - Op. Blue
— sm. piece - Irridescent White
— sm. piece - Op. Yellow
— sm. piece - Op. Green

Refer to page 18, project 9 for clock specifications.

— sm. piece - Strky Red
— sm. piece - Opal avocado
— sm. piece - Red
— sm. piece - Opal Peach
— sm. piece - Lt. Op. Green
— sm. piece - Dk. Op. Green
Mirror Border— Op. Beige

Refer to page 18, project 9 for mirror specifications.

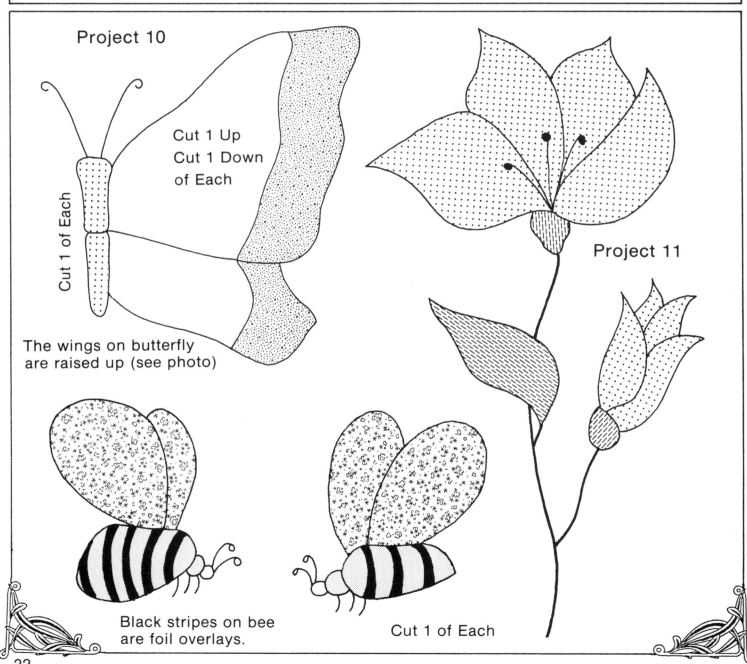

Project 10

Cut 1 Up
Cut 1 Down
of Each

Cut 1 of Each

The wings on butterfly are raised up (see photo)

Project 11

Black stripes on bee are foil overlays.

Cut 1 of Each

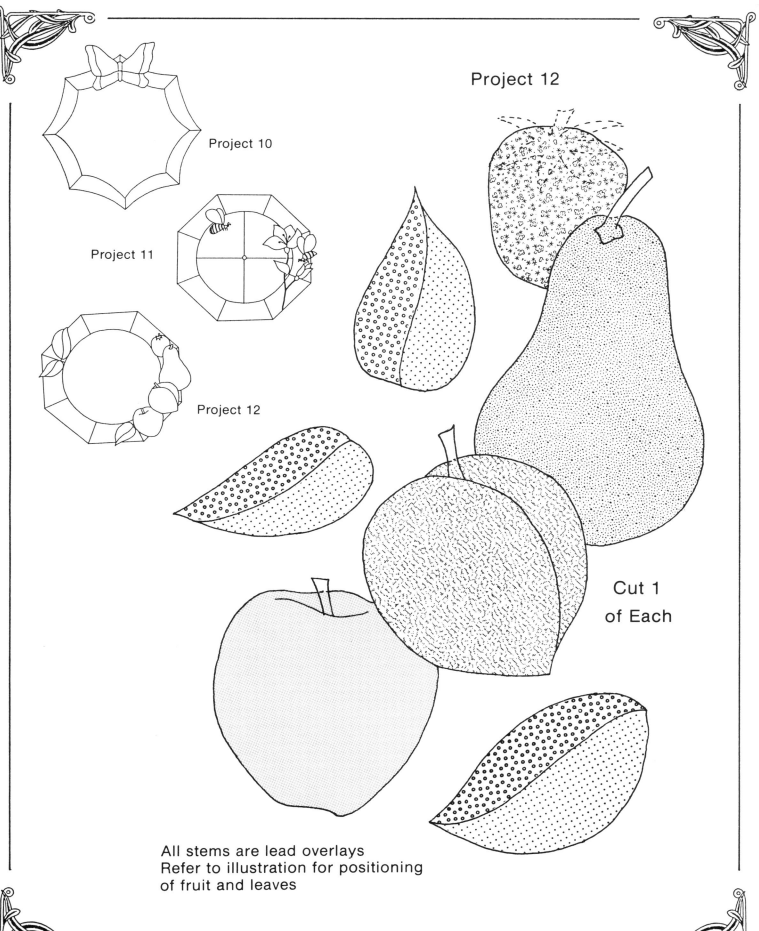

Project 10

Project 11

Project 12

Cut 1
of Each

All stems are lead overlays
Refer to illustration for positioning
of fruit and leaves

Summer Flower	SKILL LEVEL- Beginner	Project 13

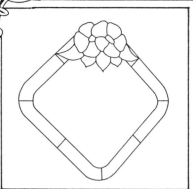

Summer Flower Overlay

Pieces— 15

- ▨ — 1/3 sq. ft. — op. pink
- ▤ — ¼ sq. ft. — Dk. Op. Green
- ⬚ — sm. piece — Op. Yellow

Project pattern on page 25

Mirror

Square Mirror

pieces — 9

Border — 1 sq. ft.
 — Aqua Op. Green

Mirror — 15¾"x 15¾"

Project Pattern is on insert page, Project 25.

Special Instruction— The hanging wire is at a corner so mirror can be hung as a diamond.

Water Lily	SKILL LEVEL- Beg./Int.	Project 14

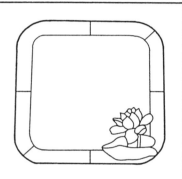

Water Lily Overlay

Pieces— 19

- ⬚ — ¼ sq. ft. - Med. Op. Pink
- ▨ — ¼ sq. ft. - Stky. Op. Green
- ▬ — sm. piece - Dk. Purple

Project pattern on page 26

Mirror

Square Mirror

pieces — 9

Border — 1 sq. ft.
 — Aqua Op. Green

Mirror — 15¾"x 15¾"

Project Pattern is on insert page, Project 25.

Special Instruction— The Water Lily can also be an overlay for the Octogan clock/mirror/frame, page 18, Project 9.

Ballerina Slippers	SKILL LEVEL— Int.	Project 15

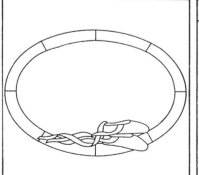

Ballerina Slippers Overlay

Pieces— 15

- ⬚ — ¼ sq. ft. - Med. Op. Pink
- ▤ — ¼ sq. ft. - Irredescent Op. White
- ⬚ — small piece - Lt. Op. Pink

Project pattern on page 26

Mirror

Small Oval Mirror

pieces — 9

Border — ¾ sq. ft.
 — Op. Beige

Mirror — 11"x 15"

Project Pattern is on insert page, Project 27.

Special Instruction— The slippers can also be used on the octagon mirror/clock/frame, page 18, project 9.

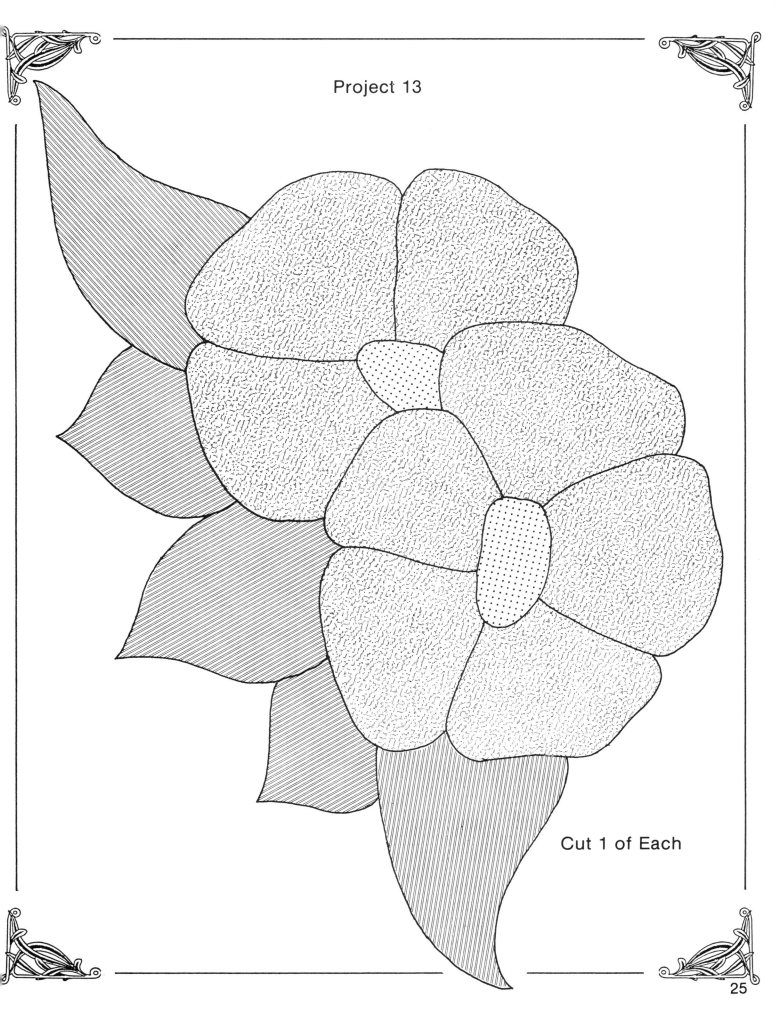

Cut 1 of Each

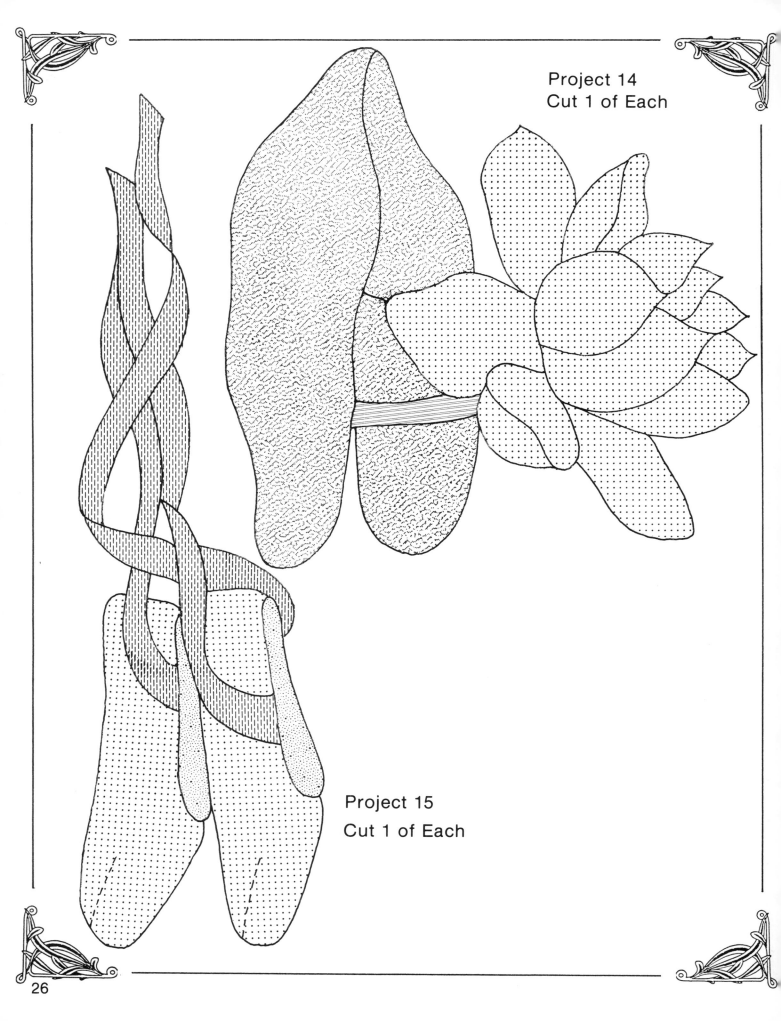

Project 14
Cut 1 of Each

Project 15
Cut 1 of Each

26

The Jag Clock | SKILL LEVEL— Int. | Project 16

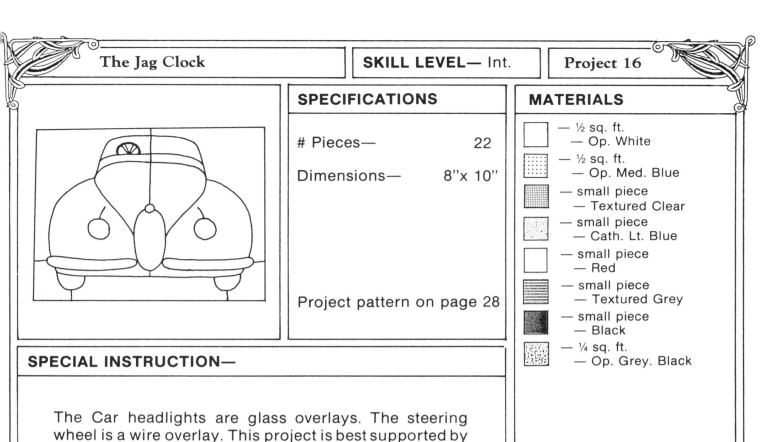

SPECIFICATIONS

Pieces—   22

Dimensions—   8"x 10"

Project pattern on page 28

MATERIALS

- — ½ sq. ft. — Op. White
- — ½ sq. ft. — Op. Med. Blue
- — small piece — Textured Clear
- — small piece — Cath. Lt. Blue
- — small piece — Red
- — small piece — Textured Grey
- — small piece — Black
- — ¼ sq. ft. — Op. Grey. Black

SPECIAL INSTRUCTION—

The Car headlights are glass overlays. The steering wheel is a wire overlay. This project is best supported by a wood frame.

Tennis Racket Mirror | SKILL LEVEL— Beg. | Project 17

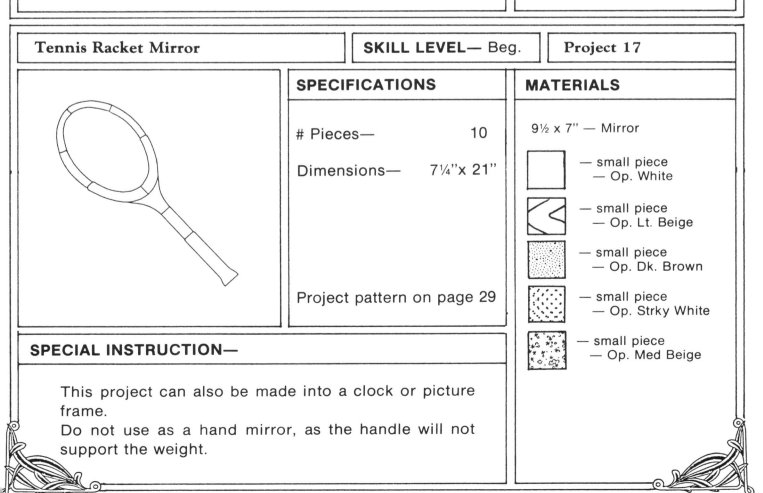

SPECIFICATIONS

Pieces—   10

Dimensions—   7¼"x 21"

Project pattern on page 29

MATERIALS

9½ x 7" — Mirror

- — small piece — Op. White
- — small piece — Op. Lt. Beige
- — small piece — Op. Dk. Brown
- — small piece — Op. Strky White
- — small piece — Op. Med Beige

SPECIAL INSTRUCTION—

This project can also be made into a clock or picture frame.
Do not use as a hand mirror, as the handle will not support the weight.

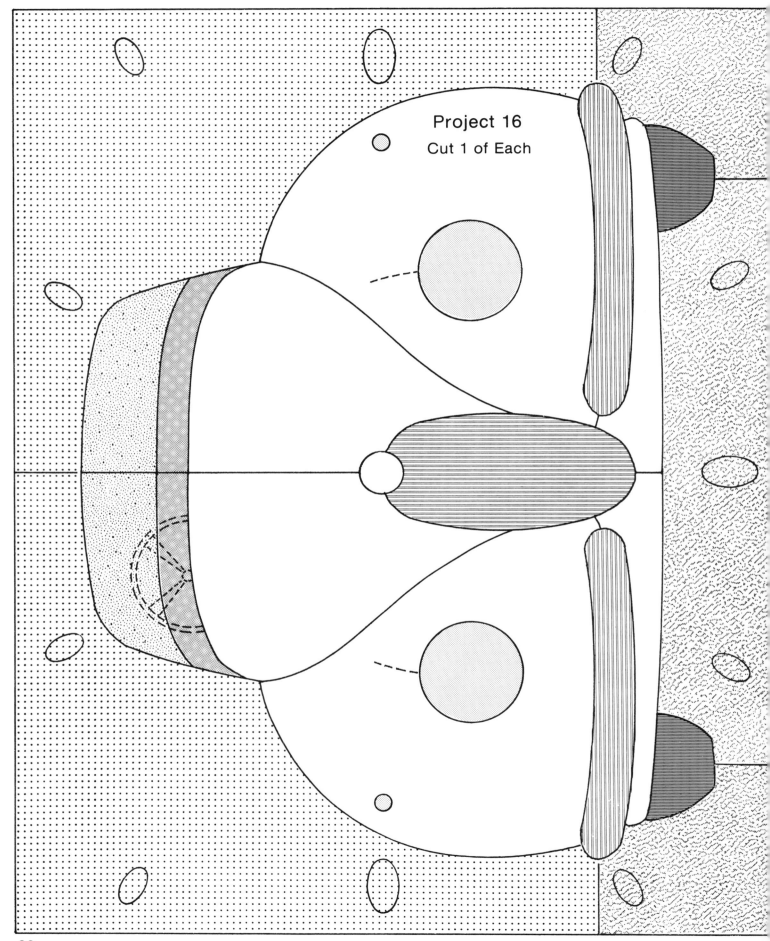

Project 16

Cut 1 of Each

28

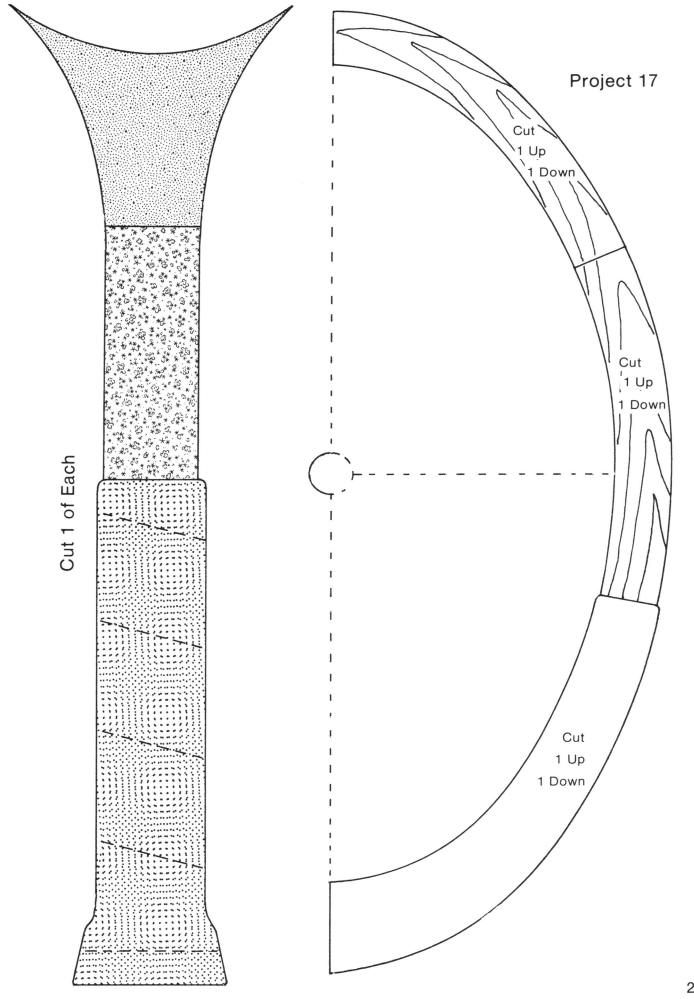

Cut 1 of Each

Project 17

Cut
1 Up
1 Down

Cut
1 Up
1 Down

Cut
1 Up
1 Down

29

Spider Plant | SKILL LEVEL— Int. | Project 18

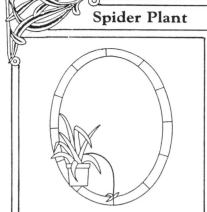

Spider Plant Overlay

Pieces— 15

Flower — ½ sq. ft. Med. Opal Green

Flower Pot — 3½"x 4½" — Opal Beige

Project pattern on page 31

Mirror

Medium Oval

pieces — 13
Border — 1¼ sq. ft. — Opal Rust
Mirror — 15"x 21"

Project Pattern is on insert, Project 28

Open Rose | SKILL LEVEL— Int. | Project 19

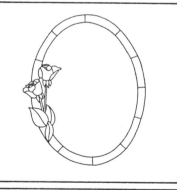

Open Rose Overlay

Pieces— 19

Flower — 1/3 sq. ft. — Opal Yellow

Leaves — ¼ sq. ft. — Med. Opal Green

Project pattern on page 32

Mirror

Small Oval

pieces — 9
Border — ¾ sq. ft. — Opal Beige
Mirror — 11"x 15"

Project Pattern is on insert, Project 27.

Long Stem Rose | SKILL LEVEL- Int./Adv. | Project 20

Long Stem Rose Overlay

Pieces— 29

Flower — 1/3 sq. ft. — Med. Opal Orange/Red
Stem — sm. piece — Opal Brown
Leaves — 1/3 sq. ft. - Dk. Opal Green
Sm. Leaves— sm. piece - Med. Opal Green

Project pattern on page 32

Mirror

Medium Oval

pieces — 13
Border — 1¼ sq. ft. — Lt. Green Opal
Mirror — 15"x 21"

Project Pattern is on insert, Project 28.

Wild Flowers | SKILL LEVEL- Int./Adv. | Project 21

Wild Flower Overlay

Pieces— 42

— ½ sq. ft. — Lt. Op. Blue
— ¼ sq. ft. — Dk. Op. green
— ¼ sq. ft. — Lt. Op. green
— 1/3 sq. ft. — Dk. Op. Blue
— sm. piece — Op. Yellow

Project pattern on page 33.

Mirror

Large Oval

pieces — 13
Border — 1½ sq. ft. — Opal Irredescent White
Mirror — 20"x 28"

Project Pattern is on insert, Project 29.

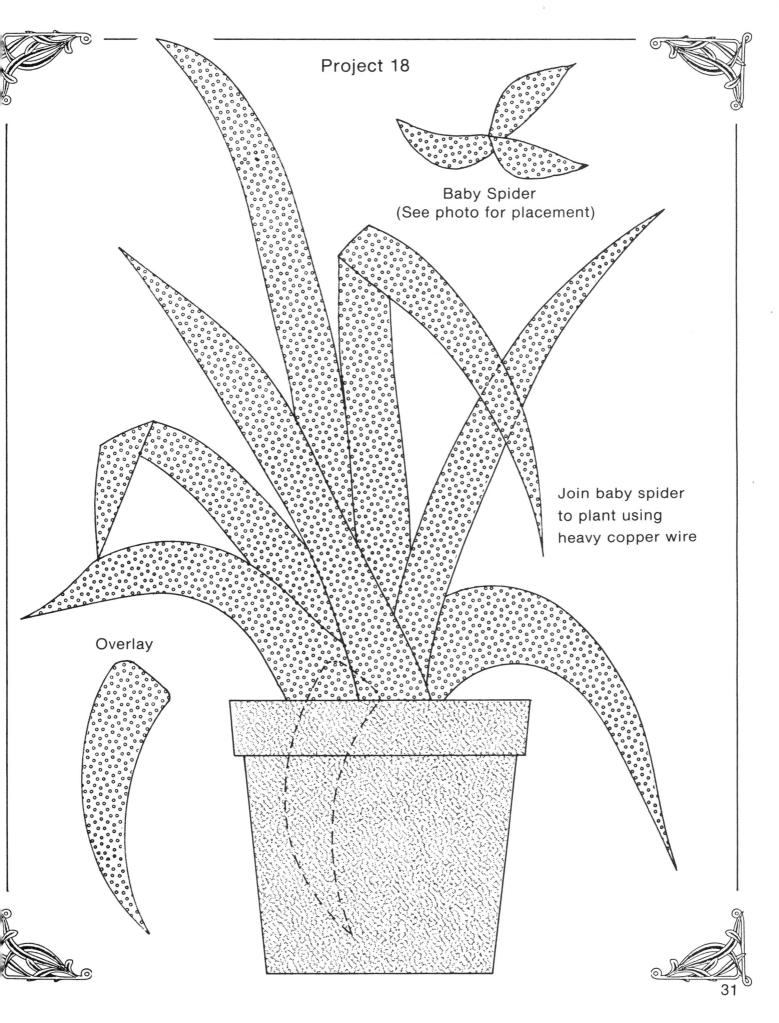

Baby Spider
(See photo for placement)

Join baby spider
to plant using
heavy copper wire

Overlay

Project 20

The --- indicates wire overlays.

Cut 1 of Each

Project 19
Cut 1 of Each

32

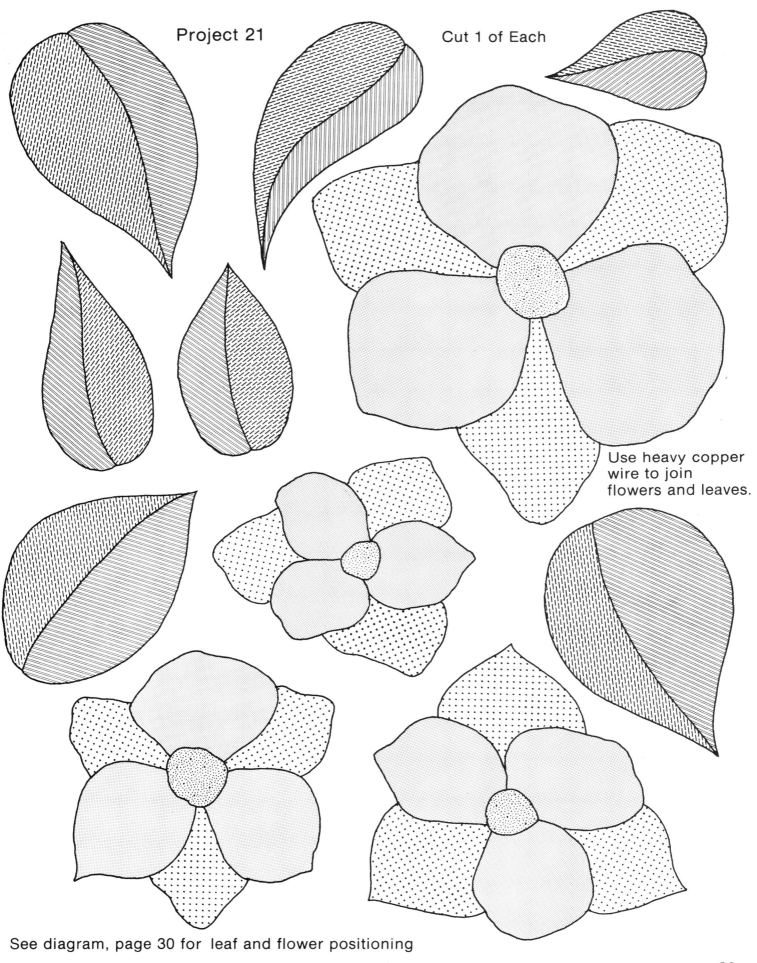

Project 21

Cut 1 of Each

Use heavy copper
wire to join
flowers and leaves.

See diagram, page 30 for leaf and flower positioning

Granddaughter Clock

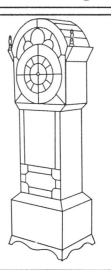

SPECIFICATIONS

Pieces—   84

Dimensions—
     Height — 30½"
     Width — 8¾"
     Depth — 7"

Clock movement requires pendulum.
Pattern is on insert page.

MATERIALS

 — 8¾ sq. ft. Dk. Opal Brown

 — ½ sq. ft. — Op. White

 — ¼ sq. ft. — Amber

 — 1½ sq. ft. Strky. White.Beige

 — 6"x 8" Antique Clear

 — 3"x 6" Flashed Red

SPECIAL INSTRUCTION—

We have attached a tall brass finnel to each side ledge at top. (See diagram.) Cut clock back using the outside 'perimeter' of clock front pattern. The space behind the clock part can be left open or a hinged door can be attached.

Fan & Vase Diptych

SPECIFICATIONS

Pieces—   110

Dimensions—   14½"x 20"
             Per panel

Pattern is on insert page.

MATERIALS

Mirror — 17"x 26"
— 3 sq. ft. Irrid. Opal White
— 1½ sq. ft. — Op. Grey
— 1/3 sq. ft. Dk. Op. Green
— ¼ sq. ft. - Lt. Op. Green
— 1/3 sq. ft. - Dk. Op. Blue
— small piece Lt. Op. Blue
— small piece - Dk. Purple
— ¼ sq. ft. — Op. Pink
— ¼ sq. ft. — Cath. Pink
— small piece Textured Clear
— small piece - Dk. Brown
— 1/3 sq. ft. Strky. Opal Green
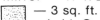 — ¼ sq. ft. - Strky. Green/Brown

SPECIAL INSTRUCTION—

For support, it is advised to use a wood or metal frame.

Colors continued...
 — sm. piece — Dk. Op. Blue
 — sm. piece — Op. Red
 — 2/3 sq. ft. — Op. Yellow

School House Clock

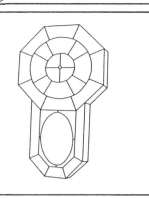

SKILL LEVEL- Adv.

Project 24

SPECIFICATIONS

# Pieces—	43
Dimensions—	10¼"x 17½"

For project pattern, refer to insert, project #24.

MATERIALS

- — 2 sq. ft.— Streaky Opal Brown
- — 2/3 sq. ft.— Opal Beige
- — 4"x4"— Opal White
- — ¼ sq. ft.— Clear Gluechip

Back piece — 7"x 9½" — Bronze Mirror

- — 4"x 6" — Oval Bevel (with a design opt.)

Special Instruction— Oval bevel can be substituted with clear glass. Top section of clock is the Octagon Clock/Mirror/Picture Frame.

Square Mirror

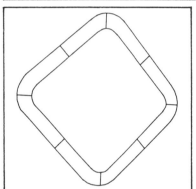

SKILL LEVEL- Beg.

Project 25

SPECIFICATIONS

# Pieces—	9
Dimensions—	15¾"x 15¾"

For project pattern, refer to insert, project #25

MATERIALS

- — 13½"x 13½"— Mirror
- — 1 sq. ft.— Aqua Green Opal

Special Instruction— For project overlays, see page 24, projects 13 and 14.

Cherry Clock

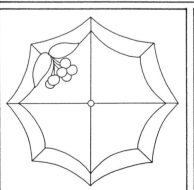

SKILL LEVEL- Beg/Int.

Project 26

SPECIFICATIONS

# Pieces—	20
Dimensions -	12"x 12"

For project pattern, refer to insert project #26.

MATERIALS

- — 2/3 sq. ft.— Opal Pink
- — 1 sq ft – Opal White or Mirror
- — sm piece — Red
- — sm piece — Opal Green

Special Instruction— This project can also be a mirror. See page 22, project 10.

Small Oval

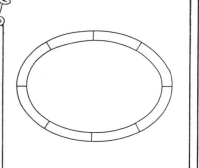

SPECIFICATIONS

# Pieces—	9
Dimensions—	15½"x 11"

Pattern is on insert page.

MATERIALS

Border — ¾ sq ft.

Mirror — 11"x 15"

Special Instruction— Project overlays are on page 24, project 15 and page 30, project 19.

Medium Oval

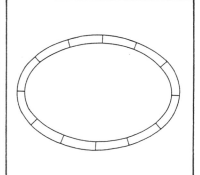

SPECIFICATIONS

# Pieces—	13
Dimensions—	22"x 16"

Pattern is on insert page.

MATERIALS

Border — 1¼ sq ft

Mirror — 15"x 21"

Special Instruction— Project overlays are on page 30, project 18 & 20.

Large Oval

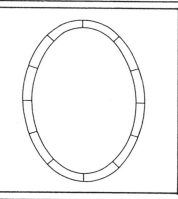

SPECIFICATIONS

# pieces—	13
Dimensions—	29"x 22"

Pattern is on insert page.

MATERIALS

Border — 1½ sq. ft

Mirror — 20"x 28"

Special Instruction— Project overlay is on page 30, project 21. It is best to mount this Mirror with mirror clips for plate glass (available at commercial glass stores).